Also by Christian Wiman

POETRY

Survival Is a Style

Hammer Is the Prayer: Selected Poems

Once in the West

Every Riven Thing

Hard Night

The Long Home

PROSE

Glimmerings: Letters on Faith Between a Poet and a Theologian
(with Miroslav Volf)

Zero at the Bone: Fifty Entries Against Despair

He Held Radical Light: The Art of Faith, the Faith of Art

My Bright Abyss: Meditation of a Modern Believer

Ambition and Survival: Becoming a Poet

TRANSLATION

Stolen Air: Selected Poems of Osip Mandelstam

ANTHOLOGY

Home: 100 Poems

Joy: 100 Poems

*The Open Door: One Hundred Poems, One Hundred Years
of Poetry Magazine* (with Don Share)

The Dance

The Dance

Poems

CHRISTIAN WIMAN

FARRAR, STRAUS AND GIROUX

NEW YORK

Farrar, Straus and Giroux
120 Broadway, New York 10271

EU Representative: Macmillan Publishers Ireland Ltd, 1st Floor,
The Liffey Trust Centre, 117–126 Sheriff Street Upper, Dublin 1, D01 YC43

Printed in the United States of America
First edition, 2026

Library of Congress Control Number: 2026938185
ISBN: 978-0-374-61740-0

Designed by Gretchen Achilles

Our books may be purchased in bulk for specialty retail/wholesale, literacy,
corporate/premium, educational, and subscription box use. Please contact
MacmillanSpecialMarkets@macmillan.com.

www.fsgbooks.com
Follow us on social media at @fsgbooks

10 9 8 7 6 5 4 3 2 1

For my mother
Frances Helen Wiman

Contents

The Dance

Emberling, amberman
worshiper of was

I asked the past
what I was meant to learn

and the past said
Burn

I.

Drinking the Bees

As if in moments
lay plummets
down which a puttering soul
might stunningly plunge

to a sun-splashed terrace
in Marrakesh:
tea so thick with mint
it conjures kelp

in a cylinder of sea
but for the bees
gauzing the top:
and the man my guide

so unperturbed
he seems to sip
from very fur
serene even as one

clings to his beard
and peers
with its tiny interstellar eyes
and fuzzed Confucian face

so near the lips
it could be the bee's
boisterous bonhomie
urging *Drink, lad, drink*

before I blink
back to Hamden
with a permanent thirst
and the sting of dreams.

The Cage

One night a week now she trades the stage
for an eight-by-eight-foot animal cage
suspended over a lacquered throng
of bodies embodying light and song

and something else she half-creates, half-perceives
as in the thump of bass and blood she leaves
self-doubt, self-taste, and self itself behind
in a slash of flesh and form and mind

opening the native gazes even of
those lost in their own mazes of unlove,
whirlwinding whirlwind reality
from which, and for which, she is free.

Out of Time

I sang the small waters
that trickled from the farmhouse gutters
and eased the jigsawed creekbed
out of time.
          I lived
into and by means of
a particular and inchoate love
that moved through the dun-tipped cattails
and the unseen red-winged blackbird
pouring forth its electronic trills
and the hill-faced bullfrog's trails
of slime.
          Memory isn't.
The images that recur
and testify they were—
the postbox's painted name,
the rust-pocked worm trough
or the storm cellar's lid of tin
blazing specific sun—
are dreamsakes the keeper claims
as a world, once more, comes undone.

To the gravid heron
oaring the shoreless blue,
for the child now cracked and creased
as a creekbed in the mouth of drought,
and with the breath of earth and earthen stone
flung to sun

when the cellar opens,
I sang, to attend, to atone.

One Hundred Years of Solitude

after the death of a disabled child

The pain of the pleasure he took
drinking coffee with an open book
and no one needing in the wheelchair near
dead legs to rub or tubes to clear
or merely for a father's eyes
once more to recognize
the word inside the wordlessness
or the glamour of a summer dress
shocks as at the back of the throat
a scald that suddenly one can't swallow
or like a cut before it starts to bleed.
He swallows. And begins to read.

for Sam Gold

In the Time of Fire

She had a vision of the vowels of doves
floating like snow in a common dawn,
not so much freed from gravity, she said,
as in league with it, a slow, deliberate dance
of chance and law.
She spoke of loneliness as a kind of sleep,
nocturnal sorrows that mark the mind
as lightly and palpably as prints in damp sand.

We cannot eat an image, we cried.
Say it: What must we do to be saved?

There was a man, she said, who all one night
beside a lake that glimmered darkly kneeled
because within him there worked
some stricken and almost animal thing
whose need, he knew, he was. He stilled his heart.
He willed away the small rustlings and retreats
behind him with the thought, he thought, of God.
But when the dawn resolved, and the lake enlightened,
uneasily he rose, pierced by the thirsts
that he had hindered.

A rumble went among us, glancingly,
like a flame flickering limb to limb in a stand
too wet to catch.

Remember the arctic eyes and pain-seamed face
of the old woman selling flowers on the subway?
The girl so glowing she seemed a nimbus of herself?
Remember the rain that random afternoon
plock plocking on the roof above you where you lay,
matching the lassitude that it released?
Look hard enough, look lightly enough,
and the un-looked-at world looks back at you.
That reciprocal seeing is the site of soul.

And the man, we clamored, who set himself ablaze
outside the embassy, that animate lick and jag
that danced him back to ash? And the shining child
crushed in the push for flour? Are these lights to light
the caves of our unconsciousness?

Darkness then. She led us to a steep bluff
that overlooked the blister city
with its maddening sanity of high-rises and highways
black lattices of train tracks like legible scars
row after row of lights implying lives each seeking to be
itself in a mud of dread and wasted days and said
within affliction there remains a space,
within that space a means of reaching free,
a solidarity of solitudes
forged and refined by the fires that are ours.
A soul can die, but it requires consent.

Beneath us glittered the endless city.
Above us struggled the unpolluted stars.
It's time, she said, you are ready, and vanished back
into the multitude before we could think
to ask who we were, or for what.

Year

(SUMMER)

Ever the river wanting what it has,
tugging and tugging at these fever trees
that never leave, the jeweled buildings
that waver, and glitter, and waver, and stay.

*

(FALL)

The season itself a sentience,
flamboying the outer banks,
leaf-clad, lissome,
outstaring the Socratic rocks,
acing the creek's curriculum.

*

(WINTER)

Crispings, icelight, January's stiletto hauteur;
some last elaborate lavish of *pure*.

*

Sunlight delighting itself on the winking creek,
exploding off the champagne glass and wedding ring
like sparks from the anvil of everything.

The Word

Writ to wonder on an old candlestick,
one word inscribed with a fingernail.
She untwists the twisted unused wick.
The flame struggles but does not fail.

Love the word and love the wish
that all day long in the parlor glows.
Love the letters that slowly vanish.
Love the nothing that alone she knows.

Before the Bone Marrow Transplant
CHRISTMAS 2022

It is Christmas 2023.
I am me, sitting in my studio looking over these notes.
An early snow (for atmosphere) floats
—clear, spare—through the bare limbs of the oak tree,
lightly and precisely redefining its guise.
The silence is such as makes one realize
silence never is, this hum the mystics call eternity.
Behind me a vast tranche of suffering lies,
in both senses: reality
I have endured and assimilated as I can,
extracting from pain a keener means to see; and,
strict formulation that says,
for all the beauty there is, for all this quick of limb and eyes
merged and made available to mind,
it is suffering that makes it shine.
Soon my wife will stir,
sunlight, because I see it, cherishing her
as she emerges from sheets and begins to dress.
My children will wake to what they think is godless joy
texting me to come down to Christmas
Now, Now
and I will think back to Christmas as a boy
and how, amid much suffering, for a time all was instant
and bright surprise. This will be done,
poem, prayer, piece of being, the tiny and entire story
of the passionate transitory in which our lives are hung.
I in my undominion rising to be among.

Moment

for Greta

The little girl who can trill her *r*'s
trills them through the dusk like a liquid engine.
He who's lost the love that moves the stars
steps out of himself as from a dungeon.

Commencement

The very day Anne died, before I'd heard,
she brisked right through me on crowded Chapel Street:
sixtyish, still wren-quick, crystal-syllabled,
so English even her sneezes were polite.

This isn't a barnyard, son, John muttered
that evening I slouched down to dinner with bare feet.
Indeed. Outside, Oxford, where long ago they'd met,
even through its mystic grays and secret mists, glittered.

Today I felt the shadow of the wing of madness,
I first thrilled to in that postmodern eighteenth-century mews
they'd leased so John could plumb the History plays,
accommodating me, my Olivetti, and my ambitious sadness.

Shoulder to shoulder at the sink each dusk,
we sudsed our separate reticences
to local markers we could trust:
foxgloves and bluebonnets, badgers and fire ants

that when I told her would eat whole birds
she shivered goose bumps I could see.
Peace, chewet, peace! John bellowed,
snapping his dish towel like a whip at me.

I'm so glad we got to be part of that time of your life,
she wrote me once, as if life had times,
as if there weren't some latent consonant grief
as ineluctable as rhymes

or genes that one day dictate
you run through sleet in an evening gown to stop a war
or veer home in some brand-new galleon of a car
or simply sit, month after month, with your mute fate.

Time stilled and belled on Chapel Street.
Motionless the man that in the shop glass blurred:
sixtyish, still innocent, if that's the word,
still chasing some old idea of "great"

(old running shoes beneath his cap and gown)—
when through that glassy ghostly self
there passed a waver like a warp of sound
that was—I heard it—Anne's live enchanting laugh:

It's barnyard all the way down.

Holding an Earthworm at Fifty-Eight

To bear the horror
of my eight-year-old arm
up to the elbow
in the worm trough,

the oily, eely
under of it all,
the viscid seethe
and seemingly imminent

clutch—
was to earn
the stern encouragings,
the gruffs and half-laughs

of the men
who've been
in that rich slither
so long by now

I'd almost forgotten how
it feels to feel
myself the center
of such tender

attention,
not to mention
the vital chill and coil
of the prize itself,

that blind writhe
that freed
as down a drought-cracked creek
a clear-stream cheer

and for a spell
dispelled
whatever it was
that made men gaze

so seemingly unseeingly
at our watery horizon,
whatever it was
that made men

men.

There Could Come a Cuckoo

So here you are, then, well past the right turn
not to mention the middle of your life's journey,
mostly acclimated to the wrathful static
your senses make as you make your way
from one errand to another, our modern furies
of emissions tests, a broken router, prescriptions
for maladies too proliferate and recherché
to keep track of, when you half-thinkingly swerve
against the you you are
to stop at one of the bespoke brunch nooks
sprouting everywhere now like some opulent acne.
You don't even believe in breakfast, much less a sweet one,
but here you are, slathering nostalgia on a waffle.
Irony's the atmosphere: jukeboxed booths, a rotary phone
for orders, even the red-skirted, white-shirted servers,
like carnal Candy Stripers, clad in past—
when it happens: the clean scalpel of a collarbone
cuts the you you used to be
wide open, and a ghost of lust goes through you like a chill.
Human beauty has its frequencies,
sunny melodies to which any sentience sings along,
remoter registers it requires a kink of character
or certain quantity of inflicted history to hear;
then rarer glossolalias of lip and chin, twilight eye
and slickrock cheek that seek some single interpreter.
There she is, chatting at the counter now,
like an eclipse you can't keep yourself from glancing at,
though you can feel the damage accruing.

There's a kind of longing that has no trace of desire,
as on a skyscraper's rooftop lookout your gut goes
right up to the edge and even over the edge,
however firmly your feet and sanity stay.
It *hurts*, her face, and try as you might the little flickers
of unlust outlast all the icy invocations
of testosterone gel, teeth-whitening strips, silver pubes.
The mock-antique clock chuckles on the wall.
There could come a cuckoo crying time
and it would hardly be a surprise. The glass sweats,
you sweat, half-melted whipped cream glosses
the half-eaten waffle like a bull's saliva.
You're gone.
There's one last thing you were meant to get,
you think, tuning the radio past apocalypse,
syrupy heartache, commodity futures, some American
and apparently transparent God who will give,
it seems, your soul's deepest need just after the ad.
What was it? And what have you done
that everyone's sounding their displeasure around you,
this cacophony of honks, screeches, curses
that even I have no idea how to end?

The One Day

When sleep was sleep and dawn was ponderable.
When idioms sillied lavish and impure
the iron integument of life itself,
and laughter tore the morning ten thousand things.
Tiny eternities of talk and touch,
explicit, unforeshadowing, light of light.
When famous suffering was just one of us,
love was license and license was law.
When evening ended. Memory was a matter
of matter. And a fastness lost to clocks.

Bug

Fractious and anxious
on the country porch
we watch some many-
angled insect like an inch
of barbed wire attached
to a gray shield-shaped plate
—the delicate filaments
of its antennae testing air
or us—touch as if with
care and keen discernment
each notch and knot
in the old wood as it senses
itself back to grass.
"This, too, shall pass,"
you say of something that,
I realize, already has.

The Dance

She wakes away a stage
    —the receding cheers—
herself some indeterminate age
    and, it seemed, known

for something she hasn't done
    in forty years.
Distracted, she oversteeps the tea
    (as she is prone),

sits in the sunlit living room,
    mines a psalm;
noticing the English ivy's
    dry and overgrown,

salvages two lucky cuttings.
    Library, bank, the gas station,
a long conversation
    with bright, unbowed Joan

at the women's shelter,
    the unspoken word *battered*
seeming to pelt her
    like a stone.

Home. A nap.
	Tidying up,
she spends an hour in an hour
	she spent at home

the evening her mother passed;
	considers "passed,"
the warm capillarial light
	in which she shone

like (she thought it) a maple leaf
	held up to sun
a long unlonelied moment
	before the day is done.

The day is done.
	She is poured out like water
but still, in bed, talks her daughter
	down on the telephone,

then lies with half-shut eyes
	stitching and unstitching
all the presences
	threaded through alone,

yielding to the slow dance
        of grace and circumstance,
a pirouette of silhouette
        and solid bone.

II.

Thunder Wonder

Thunder wonder and a dream of being
at the exact and exacting
edge of rain, happy to have myself
so mystically split yet compelled
to step into an utter
one way or another. It must exist,
that elliptical but unmistakable line
where one might stand with single mind
experiencing luck or lack
depending:
relief that rain has finally come,
relief that rain is finally ending.
If I remembered how the dream
resolved, which way I chose or whether
weather itself determined,
if I could chalk it all to metaphor
and separate tenor from vehicle,
dearth from store, it seems
some main confusion in my life
would come clear. In truth, I'm left
with that half-elated, half-depleted
feeling of coming back
to consciousness, bereft
of something I can't even name, and called
with all my mongrel words to praise
the very same.

The Eye

Among the monks was one who kept apart.
A gifted pray-er, they said of him,
who sensed my faith was mostly faith in art.
A man of fluent, fasted absences
that from his tongue would come as scalding psalms,
then yearlong silences of solid God.
A keeper of the ancient ways, they said
(which I took to mean insane) who gleaned
between the hapless captive and the called;
and that no richer privilege could befall
a stricken soul than to receive his blessing.
For seven weeks he never met my eyes.
For seven itchy, unctuous, dyspeptic,
penitential weeks he kept me guessing
where he'd be, or if the long sighs
at Mass or matins were, somehow, for me.
How could he not become my avatar
of all things holy and opaque,
with his tonsured top and mortared neck,
his gravid aspect and air of scar,
but buoyant, too, as a battleship is buoyant,
with cello legs and a cello's walk;
and a raucous root-vegetable face
out of Breughel or Bosch.
Oh—and the eye that had offended—
or so I told myself—replaced
with one of weirdly faceted glass
that even in the candled chapel flashed

a lively dialogue with light.
Some spoke of healings from his hands.
Two brothers swore they saw him levitate.
But all I saw was somber truculence,
lord so-and-so and la-di-da (though once
he hawked an egg of snot into the grate).
Unlikely—that's the word that came to mind,
like a concupiscent porcupine
(how proud I was of that one line!).
Still, I clung to what they claimed
and when the time for leaving came
sensed, rightly, that the time was mine.
He strode right up as if he knew me
and looking not so much at as through me
—as if I were a skull occluding sky—
leaned in close and whispered: *Why?*
And walked away.
I tried to laugh but only choked.
I tried to speak but had no voice.
The other monks all fawned and spoke
as if in fact some scathing grace
had driven me to my knees
and a self not mine had uttered *Please*
not knowing but knowing not to ask
if I was asking for fulfillment or release.
No. Just this pious pumpkin with his why.
Just this mild and unavailing I.
Just this low, mortar, mop-water void of sky.

I stumbled out. They closed the gate.
I didn't know if I should weep or celebrate
but felt one clear imperative: do not forget.
I vowed a higher kind of have,
a something more than memory
fusing fact and faith, world and mind
so each particular might shine
until the whole disclosed its key.
But no: the very first step I took
took something from me—that communal chant
that seemed so sad—and away was all I had.
Those days of prayer and what I'd begged,
that pumpkin monk with his cello legs
(who in truth I have embellished)
the storm-colored cassocks and tempest beards
all vanished, everything except that *why*.
That's real. Seared.
Oh—and the weird sight of his unseeing eye.

I Was Where the First Leaf Stirred

China sky, November's neural trees,
clear clairvoyant morning.
Alert, alive, in dawn's indivisible realities.
A gift. A warning.

Frosted hosta, a black trunk burled
like a half-melted candle, leaf-fall
in a locked embodiment of swirl.
A cosmic stillness over all.

Evaporates at the thought of God.
Implicates in the vise of mind.
Leaf-stir, lone bird (was it there?) pecking the hard sod.
Alone, apart, on the other side of shine.

For the Love of Wolves

Munching dust, cursing his outdated fate, he herds his
    absurdities like sheep: Prayer and Peace, Grace and God, even
    Being, *baaahh, baaahh.*

Down the valley he drives them, past the metastasizing malls
    and chemical rivers, the subdivisions of death.

Some from their secret places see him, weird beard, madness's
    mascot, with his gesticulations and imprecations, his witch-
    doctor dervishes and laughable wrath.

Some, mouthing mutton, decry silently to themselves the waste
    of time, the endless tufts of nothing on shrubs and in the
    empty streets.

For the love of wolves! they say, that being the idiom's evolution,
    evolution having reached a point of peak sheep.

Meanwhile the sheep, as unsheeplike as ever, pause to gaze in
    the windows, gathering around and behind the man almost as
    if they're herding him,

out past the city's end, the waste places, where there's no light
    but the night's sickle smile, and the incorrigible stars.

Boats

Underneath belief, its pitch and sway,
is the dark element on which it floats.
Great-Grandma, who knows Pascal
and the right whip for the perfect soufflé,
carefully crushes each broken shell
so the fairies won't have boats.

The Bond

A PARABLE

Whether the Glock that Nick was handling slipped,
or the thought he'd hardly pondered pondered him,
the trigger pulling of its own accord,
he sat oddly upright on the Goodwill couch
with half of his shocked look in his lap.
It wasn't but a blink before Miguel was there,
solid Miguel, loyal Miguel, high, sure,
but only surer high, gruffing instructions
in the phone and pressing the ocean's smell
—the Bud beach towel from yesterday!—
so lonely drunk they'd shouted smut
to the buxom clouds.
How kind the world with half a head to mind it.
And clearer, too. A joke flared and almost cohered
—*If you can read this, you're in range*—
(that sticker stuck above their jouncing truck-nuts)
before he saw—and this a shock
stark as tickle existence straight on his brain:
Miguel was crying.
"You gotta open up your heart to Jesus, Nick.
Right now. It's gotta happen *right now.*"
Bad off, in pain, his whole body caught
in a writhe that culminated in his eyes.
The bond of blood, Nick's father used to spit,
wincingly at what it cost. But love—
he stopped, wondering at the word.
Something was happening with his hands.

"Pray, Nick. I love you, man. God loves you.
Just ask. I swear, that's all you gotta do."
That dead man that dawn on the shelter's porch,
how he alone had found him, ten or twelve
or who knows how old, how even from inside
he felt the change in nature, a cold void
that everything arranged itself around,
and was. It pierced him then:
he couldn't bear what his best friend would bear,
the hell of having his best friend in hell.
And so he did. Open. Or said he did.
He closed the eye he still controlled, and,
as if the other found another means
of seeing, prayed a prayer beyond them both.
And if there was no rapture in his heart,
and speaking only seemed to concentrate
the cold, still, it felt a loving kind of lie.
They gripped each other while the siren neared,
wounded and bonded by its useless cry.

for Pádraig Ó Tuama

The Homily Asked What Heaven Was

The homily asked what heaven was,
    the choir inquired of love.
Eternity pulsed in a chance pause,
    choice light poured from above.

The two of us too *of us* to bow,
    crow hymns, weigh down a pew.
Two yeasting teens, all nudge and now,
    we slipped out, slipped off, and knew.

For some God's a gift of peace,
    For some a scathing grace.
Some know in not a deep release.
    Some, touching, touch his face.

Kierkegaard Comes to New Haven

Yale's most popular class in over 300 years.
—CNN, JANUARY 23, 2022

Church-bels beyond the starres heard
—GEORGE HERBERT

1.

The sun suns. The branches haggle over light.
An endless air of almost, these wan inveigling days . . .

2.

To triumph over life, as life has come to be:
illusory, a kind of committee tasked to live,
immured in, and obeisant to, space and time.
No refuge in the old notion of the hero.
Particularity is a greatness available
to anyone, incumbent upon everyone.

3.

Ritalin, PayPal, half-caf, binge-watch, slay, Zoom.
Precise opinions on the protein quality of quinoa.

4.

A definition of our age's irony:
to have a world replete with meaning, rife

with good and beauty, and to have a source
streaming through being like the sun through leaves,
and to not, for some weakness within, have it;
opulent, malignant, like the enlarged liver
of the Strasbourg goose, whose delectation
demands destruction of its only home.

5.

Agency, empowerment, the body, ghosted, a you problem.
A line of pug-faced buses chuffs and steams.

6.

In today's interiority we will speak of sin.
Before God in despair not to will to be oneself.
Before God in despair to will to be oneself.
The operative, obviously, despair,
though permutations spawn and spin like gnats.
To be another, shedding selves like raiment.
To chase the thing that flits and settles always
out of reach, a bird one follows far into a forest
till even the backwards back to life is lost.
Necessity: why pray to a bleak machine?
Determinism: why fret for a self the cells decide?
Fiery defiance, limp resignation, and the demon:
to hate existence, and to will one's self.

Church bells beyond the cars heard.
Undergraduates undertake the hike to Happiness 101.

Killing the Cathars, 1163

Verily each believer sucked a toad's tongue
and kissed the anus of a cat big as a mastiff.
Nor was this the nadir of their faith.
Faith? Hardly. We made them meat for ravens.
We hacked their heretic heads
and stacked their kids' limbs like kindling
for the fire in which His vengeance marvelous raged.
True, some prayed wonted prayers.
Some seemed, with their fathoming eyes
and incorrigible calm, to claim a grace
of which we knew they were unworthy.
One soul submitted his own stubbled throat
to my well-bloodied blade. *Kill them all,*
the legate said, *God will know his own.*
I didn't tremble. I slashed that proffered throat
as deftly and as righteously as all
and felt, I say, the very landscape's eye
upon me like the Kindly Light.
Why not? If by some whim or vaunt of God
one heathen heart happened to be saved,
it is embosomed now in His. That one man,
for instance—his fingercreases of dirt, his ale eyes
and specks of beard—say his heart of all hearts
was pure. What of it? Does he not gaze down
with gratitude for the blade that set him free?
Christ. That's the banner under which we rode.
Truth. That's the word no soul can shirk.
And for every killing there's a coming home.

The women weeping, kids in high glee, dogs
like wraiths among the riders, scent of meat.
The world is the world again, and the men men.

Pity the Man

Pity the man who's mastered all
the dialects of silence,
who suffers the arpeggios of snow
and in the bright kaleidoscope of fall,
as the colors combine and crescendo,
hears the oak tree plead release.

Pity the man who understands
the gift and gravity of what is not,
who lives to its conclusion
the doctrine of Saint Paul:
if being more means being less,
God's truest form is godlessness.

Pity the man whom history missed,
who, as the lie like a parasite
ate brain by brain into a single sheep,
remained immune.
Soul is the oath that he must keep,
loyal to this country called Alone.

Pity the man whose last command
comes from a cloud or a cup of tea,
his task to stand with and to withstand
the hard wind and what it blows,
to reconcile the rage in the rapist's eyes
with the power that perfects the rose.

The Word
PANDEMIC, 2020

It was an easy road but stricken with glitter,
always horizon as a vision of home.
It was vital and virtual, drowsily actual, like a cloud on water.
Change, when it came, came so soft it seemed a seem.

Now time lies on the town like a town.
The streets are empty and the doors are shut.
Consider the shiver that goes through still water like a sound.
Who would we have to be to hear it?

And God's Presence,
Will You Ever Speak of That?

for D.

How, say, in spring, quarantined,
and the air, it seemed, inhumaned,
we walked where never, and farther,
we'd been,

and under overgrown thistles
(we crouched)
that made a kind of cave
(we touched)

over moss that gave
a kind of give,
we hobbited half-laughing and half-alarmed
this was a place unmeant

for us—
until, one by one emerging
into a clearing, bits of blue
needling through needles

of high pines, we lay, the two of us,
bonded and islanded by fear
and, too, by what we hadn't named but knew
was here, somewhere,

as, high up, spooked or synced, a tree released
its shadows, two of them,
oaring over the water,
plumed, light-limned, heroned?

Deep Space in the B Minor Mass

How could he tell them that it was not silence,
the silence that claimed him even as their song soared toward God?
How could he tell them the flame that filled him
brooked no broken voice, and of a sudden
brokenness was all he was?

Somewhere in the seam between myth and memory
is the conductor's professional, undetectable
pause, his banked rage of disbelief;
the whisper-hiss traveling through the audience like a fuse;
and a song that ended for everyone but one,
whose career collapsed the instant his true gift emerged.

Amid a moment's most minor, most easily losable keys—
the leash clinks and the ice clicks,
the handslap on the back of the trash truck that means
this stink can move—
amid the cold calls and the catcalls and the calls
that you want and do not want to be
from a living God,

consider the soloist of silence,
who, while he walks his block nodding to each neighbor,
and stirs his stew to an only-and-ever-more-inward whistle,
and sits rocklike in his pew for the responsorial psalm,
keeps faith with the one moment in his life
when he had it.

III.

Not a Metaphor

As in a glass a drop of blood
spreading slowly through the water
conjures a clarity of which you weren't aware

so a people, corroded by a peace
they never learned to share,
share it only in the slaughter.

The Town

A hangman mien and a satchel full of sayso.
A whole skyscraper's cuts and cubicles
crammed into a man too short to shit
with his boots on the ground
we maybe even muttered.
Looking up at us, he looked down on us
and pronounced the town a total loss,
which we hardly needed a suit to say,
so native to it we named our teams
the Quaggas and the Auks,
who lost, of course, messily and incessantly
but with a certain sad panache
no Minister of Material Advancement
could understand. Some of us, old-timers,
recalled earlier purveyors of pragmatic despair
and counseled, with our silence, silence;
others just went on whittling,
whittling being not so much our pastime
as past time; but even those just passing through
were of a mind to feather a fellow
that efficient insufficiency
had already seemed to tar.
He set the date for demolition.
He clicked his teeth and closed his book
and revved the engine of his sleek machine.
A tumbleweed tumbled down the street
like a visible predicament.
And then there came a sign! Zeke's,

to be precise, which rattled and banged
as it always did when a hard wind blew,
as hard wind always did. This is the end,
we said, and the end is one thing
we surely own. We doused the town with kerosene,
broke the casements for the mysterious
match our ancestors left, and lost ourselves
in a kind of apocalyptic weenie roast,
searing this saying in our children's minds:
When nothing's flunkies come for you,
leave nothing behind.

Dialects and Dithyrambs

The gunned man gathers his groceries,
howdy-dos a local grandma
and scuffs to his truck.

The radio reminds him to rage.
Liver-y liberals! Like a jar of white worms,
the seethe and glop and blind imbroglio.

What the catfish relish.
Grubs, more like, reticulate as thumbs.
'Member that mammoth spelunkable mouth outta Caddo?

My lexicon surprises you, madam,
as if meat could read?
Stirruped words, yeehawing the zeitgeist.

Left on Murray right on Stone,
left right left right straight on
to the unlubricious sleep.

Who cares? Congress congressing,
Supremes with them thaumaturgical robes, crap-pants
for president, the burp and glop of a rumdumb country.

Meh, dialects and dithyrambs,
houses from the house factory,
words from the word factory,

nightminds squealing being like a slicked piglet.
He manned one once, eight years old at the Roscoe rodeo.
Like to kicked his titties off.

He giggles, the gunned man, hauls his hoard,
sweetie-pies a not-so-pliable wife,
pops a Bud.

How much do you like, he asks.
Meaning dinner.
Meaning lack.

The Watcher

for Emily Warn

As I grow older, I grow closer
To the year of fire. Deaths, loves, even the things I've made,
They fall away, or fall into, rather,
That season I stared into a sea of trees
Primed for any sign of spark or smoke.
A durable discipline: to test each intuition
Against the real. And never to lose
In beauty too acute the right regard
Or let horizon drag your gaze to gauze.
To make of loneliness a keener means
Of seeing. There is a world apart from mind,
I feel it, but what vantage past this seethe
Of cells in which we are entangled?
I played a game some days in which the clouds
Connived: childhood's elastic animals
Or midlife's imagined rapids, then great, gray brains
All roiled with one immense perplexity: me.
Until the impulse waned, and honed,
And they were merely clouds, or less or more,
Freed even from the name. I can close my eyes
And be eye level with the level hover
Of the goshawk, its brown flecks and bone frown,
The shock abruptness of its plunge
For something I can never see.
Nights sometimes I'd radio the other watchers,
All men, all fleeing something that I sought,
A feeling deep enough to flee.
I found it, finally. Or it found me.

Cleanse your vision of its mean occlusions—
Ambition, self-pity, even grief if grief
Is mostly ghost—and vision cleanses you,
As in the hush and rainlight after rain
A billion needles their single gleam,
A billion needles each intrinsic flame.
Or when the late day's reds and shadows hold
Together long enough to be alive,
Which even as you think the name—a deer?—
Melts back into the evening's embers.
Which was my last instruction, you might say:
The life a lack can hold, enable, and set free
If it becomes the lens through which you see:
I never saw the thinnest thread of smoke.
All those days I stood high in my burning perch
And watched, with all my soul, nothing burn.
This is not memory I am living in
But the end of time, in both senses,
As when a craving roving life, a life
Kindled and haunted by some clearer love,
Returns to the earth as ash, as mine soon will.
Let these words be written, then, not on stone
But as the goshawk carves the curves of a thermal
That last and lasting afternoon above the trees,
Some singular between of dream and form:
I am nature's changes now, past all change.

Haiku for Aunt Ruth

Jerky-cheeked, meth-toothed.
Dawn: strong slow puffs of grape vape.
Civilians asleep.

*

She don't sing but sang
miles of hellish melody:
all the hell he'd done.

*

The girl's piston knees.
"Reminds me so much of me."
Italicized smiles.

*

"An un-nun," she laughs.
Yet some cells are relevant.
Clang awake. Recur.

*

The kids want stories.
The past wants silence. The end?
Stories of silence.

*

An eye trained on trash.
Today's haul: a heart magnet.
Slashed, crushed. But its grip!

Good Fences

Five foster sorrows sitting on a wire.
Each caws as if on cue.
Home is the name for what the eyes acquire
when the birds,
which were always only birds,
depart, fist-sized, first, vague mites,
then disappearing from view.

Studio, 4:00 p.m.

Thinking of an old man I loved who died drinking tea.
Twenty-five years ago. A young girl, today, crawling out of herself,
as they say, as if that were possible, as if confinement
weren't precisely the problem. Raked and bagged, raked
and bagged, a season's leaves. Lunch with friends, six feet
of snow in Buffalo, a child auditioning for a lead, emergency
surgery in Brno, pedestrian torsos through the window
just before the brain goes blank. "More than usual, it seems."
Grief gives the lie to form. Nor is speech release.
Pushing back from the table whispering *no, no.*
Say something that will save me, say something that will save me,
I heard myself saying once, in a low-ceilinged room,
and without a sound, and to a book. Skin-picking,
they call it, her face and arms notched and graveled
like cosmic rock. Hands, that at least, large, strong,
but feminine, too, a certain flourish and tenderness to them,
and to him. Too few leaves now to block the light from my studio.
Half-read books. The dog asleep. Cup gone cold.
Thinking of an old man I loved who died drinking tea.

The Philosopher's Fall

All night shrinks to a single tree.
First light floods the gaps.
Leaf by leaf, synapse by synapse.
To dream the dream reality
is to bow down to what we know
is real, stake a whole life to it
—root and bole, soul and minute—
and let it all, like leaves in fall, go.

Of Love and Lice

When the turkey vulture
turns the dull black-red
coagulation of its head
and does not look away,
and, on their bedroom wall, each sees
an inch-thick patch of purpled mold
like Satan's crochet,
they weep for the lives
life denies,
then damn near split their dungarees
getting them shucked,
the moral being:
believe what you are seeing,
but there are subtleties
to being fucked.

Meadows, Too

These green declivities we come upon,
these easing umbers and bowls of snow,
were, scientists say, formed by fire and fear,
buffalo and deer fleeing the flames
our ancestors first learned to wield,
it being so much more profitable to trick
than seek, so much less exhausting,
less time-consuming, less bleak,
to kill than contemplate.
Here we are, then, our little when,
our hearts hard in our chests from the climb,
trying, one more time, to feel at home
in nature, whose nature's not to feel,
these verdant slopes, this winking stream,
intimately beckoning, adamantly real.

Prelude in Gray Major

Melancholy, most beautiful word,
like a sound some ancient instrument unearthed—
or earthed, its fusion of cave and cloud.

Or *cloud*, so close to *could*,
how the mouth rounds, sounds
not just the shape itself but a sky in which to float,

gentle hills, a house in the distance,
then a whole fall filled with cool sun and stuttered colors
through which one's walking,

considering the long and polar *o* of *alone*,
which has its own beauty,
and a silent *one*,

hiding like the seal I saw in the strait of San Juan
when the pod of killer whales glided past the rocks.
Another life, as they say, though there is always only one,

sound and mind so mysteriously aligned
one strains to tell if memory's foghorn is real
or if that's simply the sound that memory makes.

I was not alone, that much I know,
though no one was with me,
gentle swells, mists tearing and repairing,

and all the fine gradations of grays
like *melancholy* made visible,
holding its *holy* like a secret for the end.

Storm of Storms

My little brimstone, my tender bedlam,
doom-proofed and moon-assed
in the middle of the day, you,
whom all the lesser oblivions obey:
conducting destruction, translating rain,
wreaking joy.

IV.

Love Rhythm

Love your rhythm and rhythm your deeds,
the law of life the law of lines.
Be the cosmos the cosmos needs.
Be the song that with soul aligns.

Do you remember poetry?
The irksome chirp of the housebound cricket?
Bits of old onion skin like raptured insect?
Sandbox songs, splattered math . . .
Do you remember?

Kill indifference, the taciturn,
the flaw that in yourself is self on speed.
Be the quietus the wrong awes impede.
Be the beat, truth, that tips over its urn.

after Rubén Darío

I Tied My Spirit Up

I tied my spirit up
with little disciplines
of mince and simmer,
dust and plunge.

I separated, calibrated,
rated grinders
for their megawatts
of whir.

I hummed and rhymed,
recited and opined,
made of my days
a sonic lock

behind which there lay,
I said, no truth,
and to which there was,
I said, no key.

Said to whom?
Down the halls
and through the rooms,
into the very pith

and span of cells
the question boomed,
if silence can be said
to sound.

The Education of the Poet

I. THE CHILD'S FIRST VISIT TO THE CITY

Forever now the harlequin with his nimble tumble
the earthmover with its mouth of earth
Forever the river of knees and glances
Forever the towers of glitter

call to the man who was a child remember
vision's conspiracy of time and trance
that is and eases unconscious death.
Forever the waited train, forever the rumble . . .

Fangs and gleams decorate the concrete
built to keep the outsiders out.
Pressed into the wet, they stay,
and are a prophecy to delinquents by day,
and make of moonlight, when the car light
kaleidoscopes by, an elliptical angular flame.

To know, amid the acres of waste, lies
the one thing, and not to know what it is.
Is it enough to brave the bugstorm,
the crash of atoms, in the sodium light?
The saga dog deviling the perimeter,
whose name is Wrath?

3. HER DAY

The ticktock
drips from the hanging
plant; a picture—
the girls with painted
eyes and chocolate lips—
unaskant; tofu,
tomes on top, deliquescing
on a towel; Rosie, rubbed,
releasing half-gratitude, half-
growl; that critic who smelt
mildly of mint,
strongly of solitude
asking: *So, what's next?*
a loose doorknob, a text
to Mom; steam
wraithing the bath;
two "altogether new" (ha)
anti-aging (ha ha)
lotions on the vanity
and the sanity of small
devotions.

Nothing more of love
than to watch the bright beings
spurt across the screen
their elastic lives, their un-sad
disasters, their obstinate glee.
To press one's face close to theirs
until the curse and hurl upstairs
cackle and razzmatazz
and sync with the beak
of a duck. Oh, what luck, these creatures
come of storm, these avatars of form
and color and unconsciousness
dying back to life with a laugh.
Cuckoo wobble, tuba walk,
boing boing and the whistling thribble.
Closer and closer to the screen
until even the credits mean
just this flickering inconsequence,
this everlasting present tense.
Let face with the rake be struck.
Let the schmuck tumble down stairs
with a happy clash of cymbals.
Ring the king's head in the dented pail.
Let the lost child drop. Let gravity fail.

Geoffrey Hill

> *. . . and the Word was God*
> —JOHN 1:1

Paralyzed, the trees, bone-stark and light-struck
in late March, but the bright chastities of ice
drip by drip acceding to the burly sun.
A bird flecks from the worded scene,
arrows insolently alive across the yard
to re-instill itself on a topmost twig,
two quick curt chirps confirming choice.
These teasings of original, elemental life,
recurrence to terms like *resonance, re-enchantment,*
soul homing toward a scarred and artless innocence.
It is not faithless to stand
without faith, keeping open vigil at the site.
Amen. Often, though, for those so inclined, mind
hides ostrichlike in the soil of sound,
the rump of the real upstuck and obvious
for even the leanest aesthete to slap.
It's worse than I thought, you told me the one time
we talked, "the finest British poet of our time"
and "England's best hope for the Nobel Prize"
(bookjacket blather, your face glaring
from the entire front cover like enraged rock)
lamenting another book being pulped.
A sad and angry consolation, you called it,
poetry, borrowing the phrase as I borrow yours,
because poetry's sadness, aside from too much love

of this scathing life, is its iron and angry solitude;
its consolation the anonymities of insight,
inscape, indwellings that moved through pain
to language that anyone can use.
Intense unwasted life, so nearly at an end,
what can I say now, except Whose were you?
And the night terrors, the intransitive longings,
chance slashes of true joy, whose were those?
Dispense with the exigency, the *emergency,*
of form, the visceral and silent assent
that binds the cries, and to be sure words pour forth;
but this is compulsion, Geoffrey, not fate;
poetry, not poems. If I collude with you in this,
it is because from the crabbed obstruction
and stickle rhetoric of your late work
I have with my own want and wrath emerged,
balked, unawed, but touched, too, and nerved, moved
not by the thing itself, but by a dream of speech
wherein privation and devotion make amends.
I have written all this facing a plain white wall,
like an incarnation of absence, unstinting winter,
white ground, white sky, sunless in the neverwhere.
Imagine your own way out of necessity.
Imagine no need to do this.
It can't be gone, the bird that never was.
Reality is the unsayable, said.
There is a land called Lost at peace inside my head.

So I Write These Words

As, hard enough to bring down leaves,
lashing the panes of this nothing summer,

rain, in the rain's reprieve, glamours
the grass, the cyclone chain-link

and the plastic hammer, a man
looks up, belongs, believes—

Reading Steinbeck

—and the sorrows hardened,
and in the first light grew palpable, pliable,
and the man fashioned from his a kind of cutter,
and the woman made a rake,
and down the rows, which were the rows of time,
they moved, soiled, famished, ripped to instants,
but lifted, too, the man and the woman,
by the climbing sun, and by the breeze of heat,
and by the hard land whose fluency, for now, for no one
save those whom life had scathed to faith,
they were—

Jamesian

Porcelain, longing, and the science of small regard
estrange him even from his old companion, loneliness.
Her eyes are black as stars that aren't, some vast
pastness implied, and a present made of void.
Antique the sitting room, antique their talk,
but wholly now the notion that has taken hold.
She creams his tea, breaks a cracker in eternity.
Crewel, cruet, butter bell, rose chintz, ivory.
Outside, outsiders: an engine's insolence,
laughter, hammer, something coming down.
There are times, prevarications of the air,
a room a realm, civilities, declivities,
even the steam's in code. Laughter. Hammer.

Note in the Margin of *Moby-Dick*

There is something will not be named,
will not come into ken for all the forms
it lavishes and inhabits and leaves to be.

The sharp particulate light on the calm sea,
the leagues of teeth and neon lives . . .

Spasmodic god
        what constitutes devotion
to a vital null that will not be known?

Reciprocal seeings of matter and mind
that both evince and catalyze a kind
of love made lasting by its evanescence?
Maledictions stoked of hate so pure
it stuns the seeker back to innocence?

"By glimmers of the pain it left,
I felt more *known* than wounded in that light . . ."

Two Poets

I.

More telling than the tell of a bad gambler,
your lines, the tiddlywinking and the curlicues,
the velvet voltas of a mind too refined
for matter. One can't deny your devotion.
Squirreling verbs in the recesses of recesses,
anapesting your lover's butt,
savoring some master assonance at stool.
One to the manner born. If the gods knocked
at your door, Blandus, you would think them salesmen
and shoo them away. And why not?
Lauds gaud your aerie like a teen's trophy case.
Your signings are sighings. And yet, and yet . . .
admit it, dear Blandus, sometimes, at night, alone,
drowsily contemplating contemplation,
there creeps into your consciousness
something dangerously akin to consciousness.
Blandus! The road not taken yet abides!

2.

A plain style, Valentina?
As if one craved a cracker in the desert.
As if the recipe for the good life called for misery extract.
We've heard you read. Impressive, admittedly,
the creaks and groans, the breathlessness,
as if you had a coffin's worth of air.
And the moon-robed divinations! Plants, rocks, God,

all speak with one voice, which is your voice, Valentina,
anonymous, ubiquitous, like an intercom in Eden.
Up the lane straggle the acolytes, Maestra,
avid to spy this goddess of the garden,
the celebrity petunia and the cat called Meh.

Bad Literary Gathering

Time: Too late.
Place: Ice.
Attire: Denial.

Mostly silence, and when one speaks,
whole realms of echoes
like a tray dropped in Intensive Care.

A kind of nude gloom in which everyone sees
everyone else's death: a mortality colony.

Unspoken opinions of each other's work
batter the inside of eyes
like insects trapped at windows.
A joke, a comment about the weather: awkward swats.

Degrees of fame as of thermal pools:
this one uncomfortably hot,
now a midrange no-name kind of saliva,
and here a zone of coldness as of moving through a ghost.

Only much later, long after one has left,
does one realize one can't.

The Line

The call and cut of a wounded there.
A nowhere made of missing things.
Rambler, tumbler, shotgun casings
(a penny per), guitar (unstrung),
tongue depressor, feather, father.
To write a line devoid of feeling,
feeling something in the heart laid bare.
Not God. Not home. Not love or despair.
The call and cut of a wounded there.

Spells

—the sun a trombone's bell,
hell a melting ice in the mind;
mind, how against you've been;
sin (to mine a ruin), how obdurate, how fell;

me,
meeting the bright sun, these leaves the green
of summer summer never knew;
old skill, old skull, old addict of a fond beyond—

*

—to be, as once,
rocked in the body's raucous,
some deep marsupial sleep,
breathings, bladderings, heartbeat
like a velvet gong—
                    to wrest, from never,
the river within the river,
the lie underlying belong—

Press Only in Case of Emergency

The recipe called for tedium,
the tire store sold exhaustion.
In the dream he filled a stadium
where poem by poem fell just shy of sense.
And the crows returned for recompense.

And the crows returned for recompense
for what he could not say.
And all the sorrows of one man's life
gathered word by word
in the beak of a blue impertinent bird
that overmastered yet could cry

one note that reached the root of us.
And all the sorrows of one man's life
(which in the universe's calculus
weren't so very much),
called for improvise and a dash of wry.

Time like a skywriter belched and stalled.
Exhaustion was recalled.
And from the I that was not I
there riffed a rune that unperplexed.

And all the sense-lickers, and the eeling intellects,
and the Deuteronomists of Should
crept back into their holes.
And the crowd as one person rose
and called it good.

Balm

"The poems are a balm," the poet said,
whose ear endured,
besides the natural atrophy of any unearned gift,
history, mastery, and all the mosquito demons
of email and oil changes, underlings and overlords,
afternoons of disappointment and self-taste
too heavy and humid to move. "Amid it all,"
the poet wrote, meaning loves, meaning
deaths, meaning the lack of meaning
infiltrating even *heart* and *hoard*, *love* and *death*,
"the poems are a balm"—meaning,
in ancient days, a substance fragrant, resinous,
effective, for a time, against decay.

Acknowledgments

I'm grateful to the editors of *Commonweal, Ekstasis, The New Yorker, Plough, PN Review, Portico,* and the *Times Literary Supplement* for previously publishing some of these poems.

Christian Wiman is the author, editor, or translator of fifteen books of poetry and prose, including *Zero at the Bone: Fifty Entries Against Despair* and *My Bright Abyss: Meditation of a Modern Believer*; *Every Riven Thing*, winner of the Ambassador Book Award; *Once in the West*, a National Book Critics Circle Award finalist; and *Survival Is a Style*—all published by FSG. He teaches religion and literature at the Yale Institute of Sacred Music and at Yale Divinity School.

Poetry at Farrar, Straus and Giroux

Poetry has been at the heart of Farrar, Straus and Giroux's identity ever since Robert Giroux joined the fledgling company in the mid-1950s, soon bringing T. S. Eliot, John Berryman, Robert Lowell, and Elizabeth Bishop onto the list. These extraordinary poets and their successors have been essential in helping define FSG as a publishing house with a unique place in American letters. Today we continue to offer exciting new work by a broad range of poets from the United States and around the world.

Some Recent FSG Poetry Titles

There Lives a Young Girl in Me Who Will Not Die
by Tove Ditlevsen

The Collected Poems of Delmore Schwartz

In the Blood by Carl Phillips

New and Collected Hell by Shane McCrae

Trading Riffs to Slay Monsters
by Yusef Komunyakaa and Laren McClung

Poor by Caleb Femi

Foxglovewise by Ange Mlinko

Only Sing by John Berryman

The Poems of Seamus Heaney

Joy in Service on Rue Tagore by Paul Muldoon

ohn Berryman • Pablo Neruda • T. S. Eliot • Robert Lowell •
lizabeth Bishop • Randall Jarrell • Allen Tate • Juan Ramón
iménez • Louise Bogan • Nelly Sachs • Salvatore Quasimodo •
leksandr Solzhenitsyn • Jean Valentine • James Wright •
ermann Hesse • Sidney Goldfarb • Derek Walcott • Philip Larkin •
hom Gunn • Seamus Heaney • Stevie Smith • James Schuyler •
eberto Padilla • Killarney Clary • Les Murray • Joseph Brodsky •
dam Zagajewski • Frederick Seidel • John Ashbery • August
leinzahler • C. K. Williams • Sappho • Frank Bidart • Lawrence
oseph • Chase Twichell • Tony Harrison • Rosellen Brown •
leksandr Kushner • Robert Fitzgerald • Mina Loy • Gjertrud
chnackenberg • Michael Fried • Horace • Pier Paolo Pasolini •
vid • James Fenton • Robert Pinsky • Federico García Lorca •
irgil • Rainer Maria Rilke • Homer • Paul Muldoon • Charles
right • Vinícius de Moraes • Dante Alighieri • Eugenio Montale •
renda Shaughnessy • Giuseppe Ungaretti • Po Chü-i • Henri
ole • Grace Paley • Petrarch • Carl Phillips • Yusef Komunyakaa •
ouise Glück • Jeff Clark • Ingeborg Bachmann • Don Paterson •
ves Bonnefoy • Mahmoud Darwish • Christopher Logue • Eliza
riswold • Durs Grünbein • Michael Hofmann • Stuart Dybek •
arie Étienne • John Betjeman • James McMichael • John
lare • Richard Howard • Susan Wheeler • Maureen N. McLane •
inéad Morrissey • Joshua Mehigan • Ange Mlinko • Ishion
utchinson • Peter Cole • Leonard Cohen • Yehuda Amichai •
. E. Stallings • Patrizia Cavalli • Giacomo Leopardi • Daniel
adler • Valerio Magrelli • Ted Hughes • Michel Houellebecq •
Qingzhao • Laren McClung • Glyn Maxwell • Devin Johnston •
omas Tranströmer • Paul Celan • Spencer Reece • Carol Ann
uffy • James Lasdun • Bill Knott • Karen Solie • Averill
urdy • Katie Peterson • Robin Robertson • Gottfried Benn
Carlos Drummond de Andrade • Luciano Erba • Marianne
oore • Maria Dahvana Headley • Christopher Reid • Eleanor Chai
Charles Bernstein • Max Jacob • Christian Wiman • Hannah
ullivan • Rowan Ricardo Phillips • Sylvie Baumgartel • francine j.
arris • Shane McCrae • Iman Mersal • Valzhyna Mort •
harles Baudelaire • Chet'la Sebree • Paul Valéry • Delmore
chwartz • Roya Marsh • John Koethe • Victoria Chang • Lindsay
urner • Tove Ditlevsen • Ben Lerner • Maggie Millner •
ntonella Anedda • Jorie Graham • Declan Ryan • Oli Hazzard •
isa Gonzalez • Colin Channer • Brontez Purnell • Caleb Femi